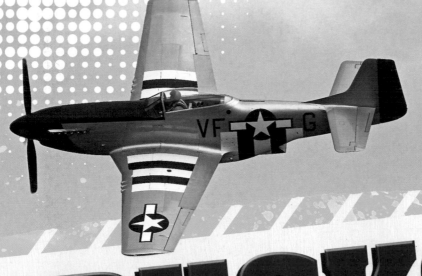

TRUCKS TRAINS BOATS AND PLANES

By Lee Anne Martin

SCHOLASTIC

Tangerine Press
an imprint of
SCHOLASTIC
www.scholastic.com

© 2013 becker&mayer! LLC

Published by Tangerine Press, an imprint of Scholastic Inc., 557 Broadway, New York, NY 10012;
Scholastic Canada, Ltd., Markham, Ontario
Scholastic UK, Warwickshire, Coventry
Grolier International, Inc., Makati City, Philippines

Produced by becker&mayer!, LLC.
11120 NE 33rd Place, Suite 101,
Bellevue, WA 98004
www.beckermayer.com

If you have questions or comments about this product, please visit www.beckermayer.com/customerservice.html and click on the Customer Service Request Form.

Written by Lee Anne Martin
Edited by Delia Greve
Designed by Sarah Baynes
Photo research by Katie del Rosario and Emily Zach
Production management by Jen Marx

Printed, manufactured, and assembled in Shenzhen, China
10 9 8 7 6 5 4 3 2 1
ISBN: 978-0-545-59364-9
12701

TRUCKS

What do the first truck, motorcycle, and taxi have in common? German engineer Gottlieb Daimler. He invented all three vehicles! In fact, by inserting his new lightweight engine into the body of a stagecoach, Daimler created the first four-wheeled vehicle.

There are many different types of fire trucks to help firefighters face all kinds of fires. A hook-and-ladder fire truck, also called a tractor-drawn aerial, is made to move through narrow city streets. These trucks have two steering wheels—one in the front and one in the back—to help them make tight turns. The truck can also pump about 1,000 gallons (3,785 l) of water per minute.

The ladders on these trucks can extend up to 100 feet (30 m) in the air (about 10 stories). They are mounted on a turntable and can turn in any direction.

ON THE MOVE

Whether you're traveling down the street, across the country, or around the world, there are many ways to get from here to there.

On the road, by rail, over water, or up in the sky—trucks, trains, boats, and planes are always on the move. Some vehicles help people work, such as trucks that dig holes, lift boxes, push rocks, and haul grain, animals, and milk. Other vehicles transport goods long distances, such as freight trains, cargo ships, semis, and cargo planes. Whether the vehicle is larger than a house, moves faster than the speed of sound, or soars high above the ground with no motor—all vehicles help us get from one place to another.

There are lots of trucks, trains, boats, and planes—how many new vehicles will you discover?

PUMPER FIRE TRUCK

This is the fire truck you're most likely to see hurrying to a fire or other emergency. It carries up to 1,000 gallons (3,785 l) of water and long hoses, but it has no ladder.

AMBULANCE

Ambulances are stocked with medical equipment.

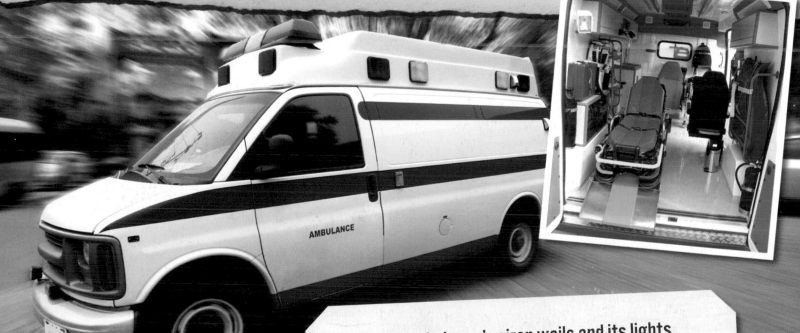

When an ambulance's siren wails and its lights flash, it's telling other drivers, "Move over! Coming through!" Ambulances need to move quickly to take sick or injured people safely to the hospital.

This machine can dig holes, ditches, trenches . . . you name it, the backhoe can dig it! With the big bucket attached to the long arm, or boom, it scoops up earth, rocks, or concrete.

BACKHOE

This is what you call a heavy-duty truck. See all the wheels? It needs all of them to move the weight of the truck and the rock, sand, or dirt it carries. When it's time to dump the load, the box lifts up in the front so the contents can slide out the back onto the ground.

DUMP TRUCK

LOADER

The loader may look like a backhoe, but the bucket on this machine is used for lifting and carrying, not so much for digging. The driver lowers the bucket to the ground to scoop a load of dirt, rocks, sand, or snow. Then the bucket is lifted and tipped back so nothing spills out. When the loader gets where it is going, the driver tips the bucket down to empty the load.

FORKLIFT

Forklift drivers often zip around in reverse, looking over their shoulders to see where they are going. That's because the loads carried on the machine's forks, or bars, make it hard to see out the front. Forklifts are made to carry stuff that's too heavy for a person to lift—from a pile of rocks to a pallet of potato chips.

ZAMBONI MACHINE

If you've been to a skating rink or hockey arena, you've probably seen one of these special machines resurfacing the ice. Weighing in at more than 5,000 pounds (2,268 kg), these machines first shave the surface with a blade and then spray water onto the ice and vacuum it up. Finally, they spread a layer of hot water on the ice to create a perfectly smooth, flat surface.

DOUBLE DECKER BUS

Being two stories high, these buses are easy to spot weaving through city streets. The first double-decker buses were pulled by horses, and passengers used a ladder to get to the upper level. Today, they have engines and stairs, and are used to give city tours, or for general transportation.

MONSTER TRUCK

Daring leaps over huge obstacles, wild races through deep mud, and bold rides up and over barriers—these trucks do amazing things! Made from regular pickup truck bodies, they are tricked out with enormous wheels that are about 6 feet (18 m) tall.

ARMORED TRUCK

With walls, floor, doors, and ceiling made from heavy-duty steel—this is one superstrong truck! Built to protect, armored trucks are the safest way to move money and other valuables—and even people!—from one place to another.

GARBAGE TRUCK

There are many types of garbage trucks in different neighborhoods. This is a rear loader garbage truck. After workers dump trash into the back of the truck, a compacting blade pulls the garbage up into the truck and smashes it tightly to make room for more.

TOW TRUCK

Who do you call when your car is stuck in mud or snow, ditch or a hole, or when it just won't run? A tow truck! These trucks use pulleys, chains, and hooks to lift the car's front wheels off the ground (the car's rear wheels roll on the road)—then it pulls the car away.

CRANE TRUCK

Some booms can be as long as 200 feet (61 m) and lift up to 100 tons (91 tonnes)!

Workers use the long arm, or boom, on this truck for extra-heavy lifting. Large metal braces, called outriggers, on either side of the truck help support it while the boom is in use.

CONCRETE MIXER

This truck doesn't just move concrete—it mixes it, too! Workers load sand, gravel, or powdered cement into the drum (the large cylinder on the back of the truck), along with water. As the truck drives to its destination, the drum turns, mixing the materials together.

When the truck arrives at its destination, the concrete is ready to pour.

BULLDOZER

Did you know that pushing dirt around is called *dozing*? A bulldozer is a big machine that uses a blade attached to the front to push sand, gravel, and dirt. (A small machine that does the same thing is called a calf dozer.) The tracks on the bottom of the tractor help it move through heavy mud or sand.

EXCAVATOR

To excavate means to dig—but an excavator uses its boom and bucket for more than digging. It can also knock down buildings! An excavator can move on wheels or tracks, and the cab where the operator sits can spin all the way around.

QUARRY TRUCK

These massive trucks are so heavy they aren't allowed on regular highways. They work in mines and quarries, moving colossal loads of rocks and stones—up to 75 tons (68 tonnes). That's over 150,000 pounds (68,039 kg)!

730E

This is the largest land transport vehicle in the whole world! Dubbed "the gentle giant" by NASA, the crawler transporter carried the space shuttle to the launch pad for liftoff for more than 40 years. At 113 feet wide and 31 feet long (34.5 by 9.5 m), it's as wide as a four-lane highway and carries 5,000 gallons (18,927 l) of fuel. But the gentle giant is a slow mover; its top speed is just 1 mph (1.6 kph).

NASA's space shuttles were the first reusable spacecraft. The shuttle is made up of the orbiter (the plane-like structure), an external fuel tank, and two rocket boosters.

USA

CRUISER MOTORCYCLE

Cruisers are heavy motorcycles made for comfortable driving, or cruising. The seats tend to be lower, the handlebars higher, and the pedals positioned slightly forward. Most cruisers have powerful engines.

OFF-ROAD MOTORCYCLE

These motorcycles are built to churn through sand, dirt, and mud—it's why they are also called dirt bikes! They tend to have a high suspension and clearance from the ground for carving turns and taking jumps at high speeds. Most off-road motorcycles are used in races and other sporting events.

SEMI TRUCK

Tractor-trailers, semis, eighteen-wheelers, big rigs—these trucks are called a lot of different names! To haul material long distances, the back, or trailer, is loaded with goods while the driver steers from the front, or tractor, part of the truck.

Some tractors have stylish cabins with excellent sound systems and a place for the driver to sleep (when they're not driving, of course!).

TANKER TRUCK

The trailer on this type of semi is a tube-shaped tank used to carry liquids, such as milk, oil, or gasoline. At almost 48 feet (15 m) long, it can carry up to 9,100 gallons (34,447 l) of liquid—that's a lot of jugs of milk!

DELIVERY TRUCK

Whether you're sending a package or having flowers delivered, it will probably arrive in one of these trucks. Since the 1920s, delivery trucks, with their sliding driver side doors, have traveled the streets of towns and cities transporting baked goods, laundry, and other items between shops and to doorsteps.

VACUUM TRUCK

This vehicle has major sucking power! Its long hose pulls up water, dirt, dust, and other debris, and deposits it into the large tank on the back. These trucks help clean up city streets, sewers, oil storage tanks, and oil spills.

These trains travel on conventional railroad tracks, but they move at much faster speeds than most passenger trains. In the US, they race across long distances going at least 90 mph (145 kph), and at least 185 mph (300 kph) in European and Asian countries.

High-speed trains typically have a power car, or a car with an engine and brakes, at both the front and back end of the train.

HIGH-SPEED TRAIN

TRAINS

Almost two thousand years ago, people noticed an interesting thing. Vehicles traveling over a predetermined, or set, path use less energy than free-moving vehicles. This idea led to the creation of "wagonways" and eventually to the invention of the train!

DOUBLE DECKER TRAIN

Twice the height—twice the passengers! By adding a second level of seats, these trains can carry more people.

Although train travel isn't exactly cutting edge, it's still a fun way to get from one place to another. In the United States, trains have been taking people where they want to go since 1830. Amtrak, the country's rail system, has over 21,000 route miles (33,800 km) and operates more than 300 trains a day.

PASSENGER TRAIN

Most passenger trains have dining cars and sleeping cars for long-distance trips.

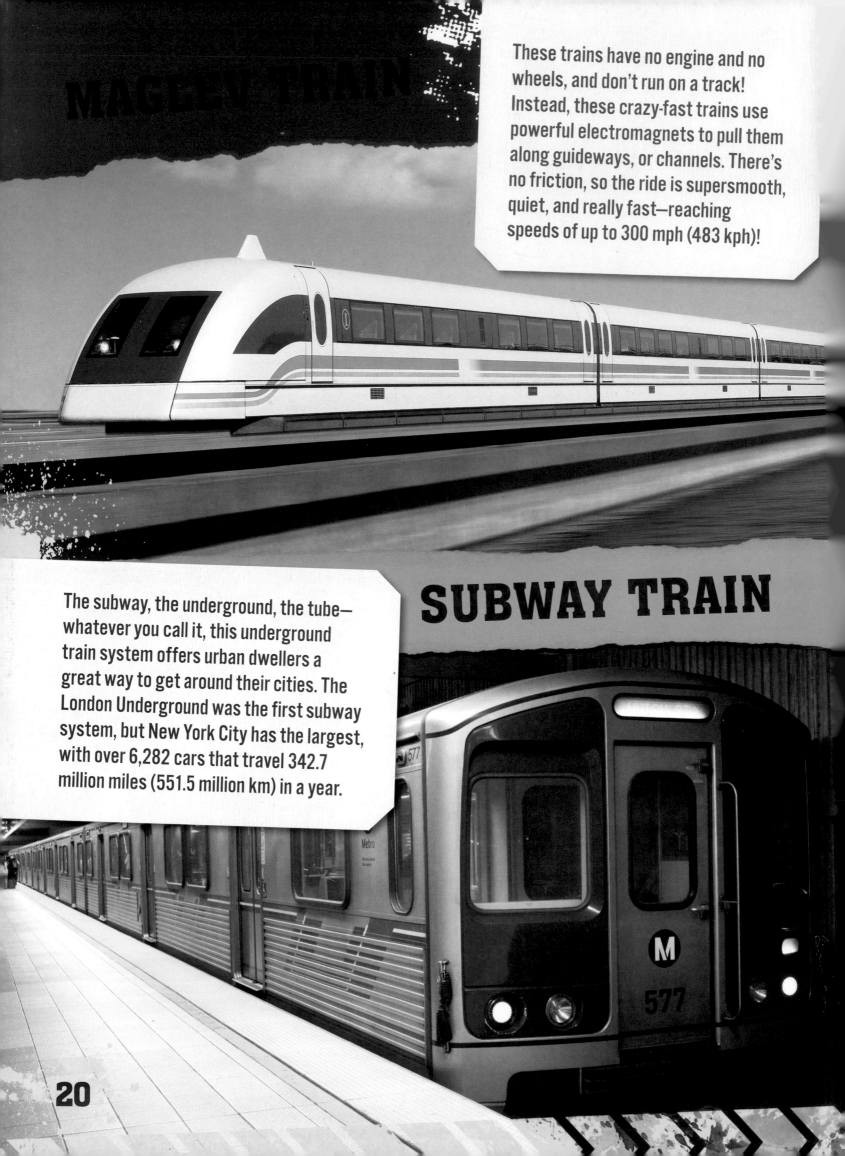

MAGLEV TRAIN

These trains have no engine and no wheels, and don't run on a track! Instead, these crazy-fast trains use powerful electromagnets to pull them along guideways, or channels. There's no friction, so the ride is supersmooth, quiet, and really fast—reaching speeds of up to 300 mph (483 kph)!

SUBWAY TRAIN

The subway, the underground, the tube—whatever you call it, this underground train system offers urban dwellers a great way to get around their cities. The London Underground was the first subway system, but New York City has the largest, with over 6,282 cars that travel 342.7 million miles (551.5 million km) in a year.

PEOPLE MOVER

You'll most likely encounter these nifty little trains at airports or theme parks. Controlled by computers rather than drivers, they efficiently transport people short distances.

TROLLEY CAR

Also known as streetcars or trams, trolleys run on rails that are set right into the city streets. The bars on top connect to electrical wires overhead for power.

21

ELEVATED TRAIN

Some trains run on the ground, some travel underground, and others ride rails high above the ground on elevated tracks. Chicago is home to one of the most famous elevated trains, called the El.

Kimball

LIGHT RAIL

Offering city folks another way to get around quickly, these electric trains travel at about 60 mph (100 kph) on street-level rails or on elevated tracks.

MONORAIL

The cool thing about a monorail train is the *mono*, or single, track it runs on. These trains straddle the track and are either elevated or at street level.

FREIGHT TRAIN

Freight is simply another name for cargo or . . . *stuff*. Freight trains carry stuff—a lot of it—all over the country. Most freight trains are about one-half to one mile long, but some coal trains can be almost two miles long! If you're counting, that's about 190 cars, each carrying about 110 tons (100 tonnes) of coal.

TYPES OF FREIGHT CARS

Freight trains use different types of cars to carry different types of goods or cargo.

BOXCAR

These cars are used to haul many different types of goods, including large and oddly shaped material. The sliding doors on the side make boxcars easy to load and unload.

HOPPER CAR

Used to haul coal, fertilizer, or grains, hopper cars can be either covered or uncovered. All hoppers have a drop-bottom chute, or door on the underside of the car, so they can be be quickly unloaded.

TANK CAR

Like tanker trucks, tank cars carry liquids such as oil and chemicals, and many types of gases. But these rail cars can carry up to 30,000 gallons (113,500 l) of liquid or gas—that's almost three times more than a tanker truck!

WELL CAR

Designed to carry shipping containers, these cars have a shallow hole, or well, in which a container sits. Well cars can carry up to two containers, stacked on top of each other.

A gear, or cogwheel, on the underside of the train engages with the middle cog rail to keep the train from sliding backward on steep hills.

COG RAILWAY

Most trains can travel over gentle slopes of four to six percent incline. But cog trains are built to climb steep slopes—those with inclines of up to 48 percent. Cog trains have an additional ridged rail in the middle of the track, called a cog rail.

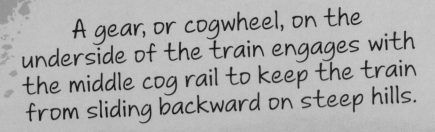

FUNICULAR TRAIN

These trains are built to climb! By traveling on rails like a train and using cables like an elevator, these trains can scale supersteep hills. The steepest funicular railway is Katoomba Scenic Railway in Australia, which carries passengers up a 122-percent incline—that's a super-steep slope!

CABLE CAR

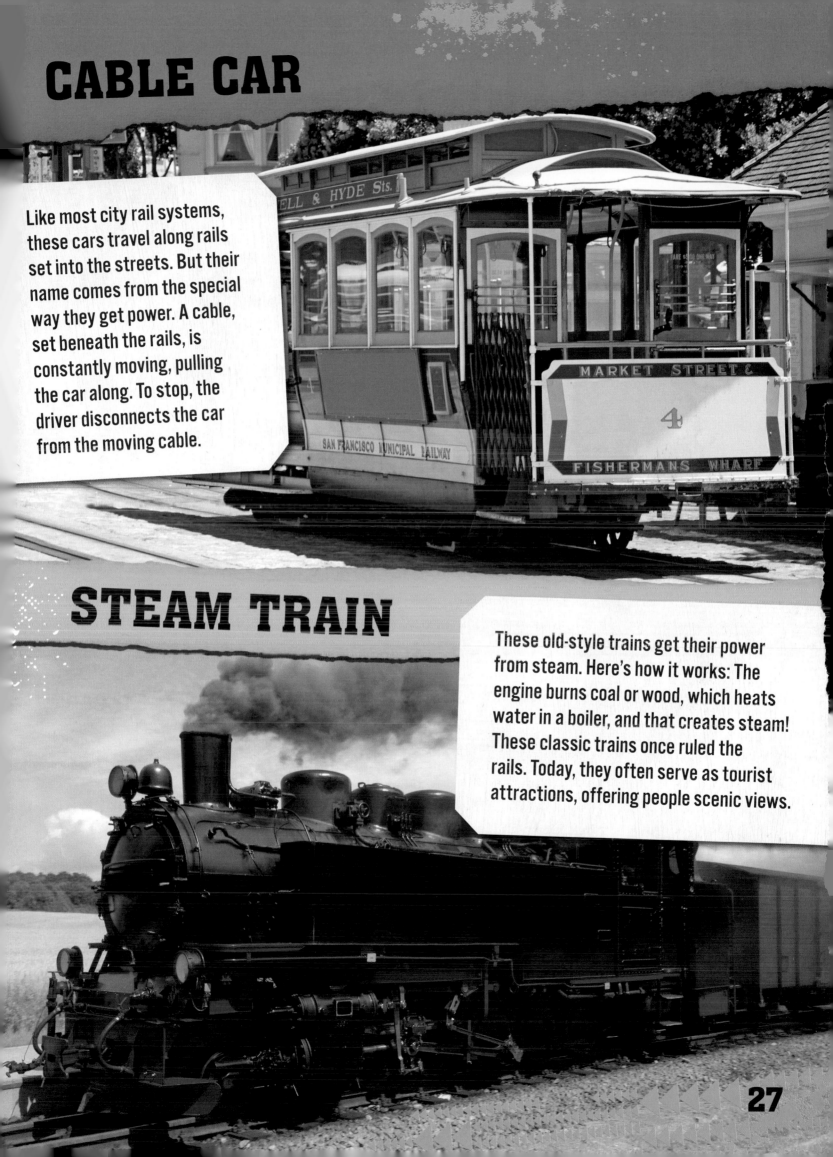

Like most city rail systems, these cars travel along rails set into the streets. But their name comes from the special way they get power. A cable, set beneath the rails, is constantly moving, pulling the car along. To stop, the driver disconnects the car from the moving cable.

STEAM TRAIN

These old-style trains get their power from steam. Here's how it works: The engine burns coal or wood, which heats water in a boiler, and that creates steam! These classic trains once ruled the rails. Today, they often serve as tourist attractions, offering people scenic views.

Because these special ships are so expensive to build and maintain, there are only 32 aircraft carriers in the world, as of 2013.

INTREPID

AIRCRAFT CARRIER

Stretching 1,040 feet (317 m) long and 20 stories high, these enormous ships have a flight deck, or a runway for planes, built on top. With up to 80 planes and between 5,000 and 6,000 sailors on board, it's easy to see why the US Navy calls these ships "the powerhouse of the fleet"!

BOATS

People have used boats for more than 10,000 years! The earliest boats were simply hollowed-out logs or wooden rafts. We've come a long way since then. With the invention of sails and the engine, the way we navigate the world's oceans has changed along with the size of the ships.

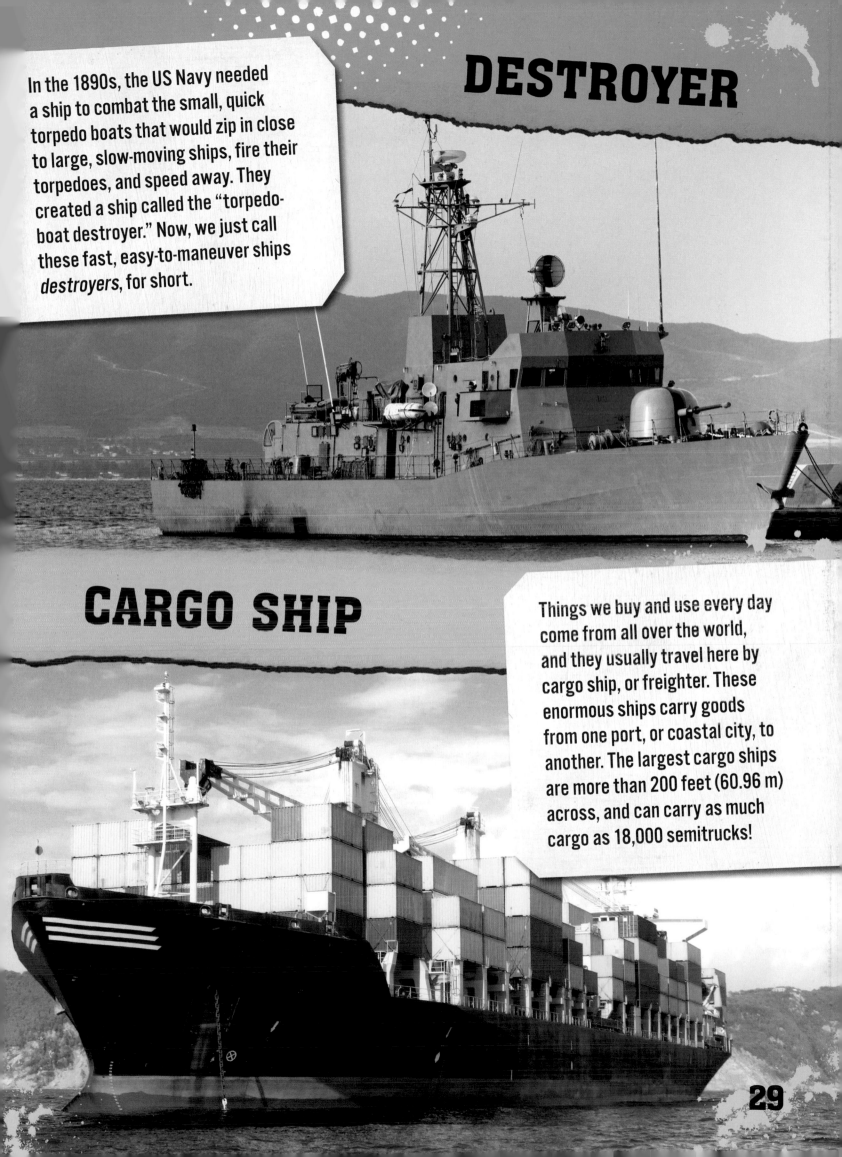

DESTROYER

In the 1890s, the US Navy needed a ship to combat the small, quick torpedo boats that would zip in close to large, slow-moving ships, fire their torpedoes, and speed away. They created a ship called the "torpedo-boat destroyer." Now, we just call these fast, easy-to-maneuver ships *destroyers*, for short.

CARGO SHIP

Things we buy and use every day come from all over the world, and they usually travel here by cargo ship, or freighter. These enormous ships carry goods from one port, or coastal city, to another. The largest cargo ships are more than 200 feet (60.96 m) across, and can carry as much cargo as 18,000 semitrucks!

BARGE

Barges are large, flat-bottomed boats designed to carry goods along canals or rivers. Most have no source of power, so tugboats, horses, or even people pull or push them along.

FISHING TRAWLER

Trawls are huge nets used to catch many fish at once. A fishing trawler is a commercial fishing boat that drags these nets through the water, capturing fish. Most trawlers have an area where workers sort the catch, tossing back what they can't use and storing the fish they want to sell.

TUGBOAT

Tugboats, or simply *tugs*, are the sturdy hard-workers of the boat world. Tugs tow and push other boats, such as barges that can't move on their own or ships that need help getting into tight spaces. Most tugboats range from 70 to 200 feet (21 to 61 m) long.

OIL TANKER

To help prevent spills, these ships typically have double hulls—one hull built inside the other.

After oil is pumped out of the ground, it is taken to a refinery to be purified, or cleaned. Oil tankers are mammoth ships used to move huge quantities of crude oil to these refineries.

RAFT

Almost anything that is flat and floats can be called a *raft*. But for shooting down white-water rapids, you want something stable and flexible. Most are made of inflatable rubber and steered by one or more paddlers. They can be from 11 feet (3.5 m) to 20 feet (6 m) long, and hold from four to twelve passengers.

White-water kayaks are another type of boat used to maneuver fast-moving rapids.

There are many different types of sailboats. Each one has a special name and arrangement of sails. A sloop has one mast—the tall pole in the middle of the boat—with two sails: a mainsail (the big sail) and a jib (the smaller sail in front).

SLOOP SAILBOAT

HYDROPLANE

To *hydroplane* means to "skim across the surface of the water," and that's exactly what hydroplane boats do . . . at super-high speeds. The fastest hydroplane hit 317 mph (510 kph). Skimming on top of water at over 300 miles per hour makes it pretty difficult to steer—so driving these boats is a big challenge!

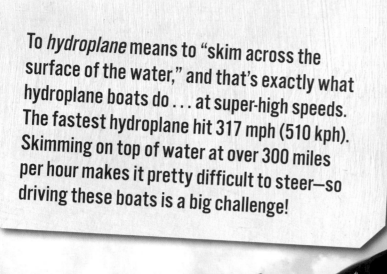

MOTORBOAT

A motorboat can be any boat propelled by a motor, but when people talk about motorboats, they usually mean a smaller boat (around 30 feet long or less) with a powerful motor.

Ski and wakeboard boats are designed to tow waterskiers or wakeboarders.

ICEBREAKER

Icebreakers keep shipping lanes, such as those in the Arctic Ocean, clear of ice. But icebreakers don't just crash into the ice to break it up. They use their extremely powerful engines to push the gently sloped bow up on top of the ice. Under the massive weight of the ship, the ice breaks apart, creating a pathway for other ships.

SUBMARINE

When submarines dive underwater, they fill special tanks with water so they become denser than the surrounding water, and they sink.

Submarines submerge, or sink, and travel underwater for long stretches of time. Their strong, reinforced hulls and the smooth, rounded shape help them handle the extreme water pressure of the deep ocean.

How do cars get across the water when there is no bridge? They take a ferryboat! Also called ferries, these boats shuttle cars, trucks, bikes, and people across bodies of water. At the dock, cars and people get on, then the ferry chugs across the water. When it lands, the cars drive right off.

FERRYBOAT

Some ferries have openings on both ends and some ferries load vehicles from the side.

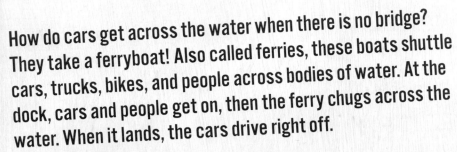

KITTITAS
SEATTLE WA

QLENACHULISH

HOSPITAL SHIP

A floating hospital! This type of ship travels along a country's coast, from port to port. People come to the ship for medical attention when there are no traditional hospitals nearby.

U.S. NAVAL HOSPITAL SHIP
MERCY
IMO 7390454

HOVERCRAFT

A hovercraft travels on a cushion of air—so, it may look like a boat, but it can move over both water and land. Some float close to the ground, and some gain a lot of height, hovering up to 9 feet (2.75 m) above the surface. People use hovercrafts on icy lakes and ponds, or to explore waterways that can't be reached in a regular boat.

FIREBOAT

When a boat or pier goes up in flames, a fireboat comes to the rescue! Fireboats are equipped with powerful hoses that can pump thousands of gallons of water per minute and spray it hundreds of feet in the air.

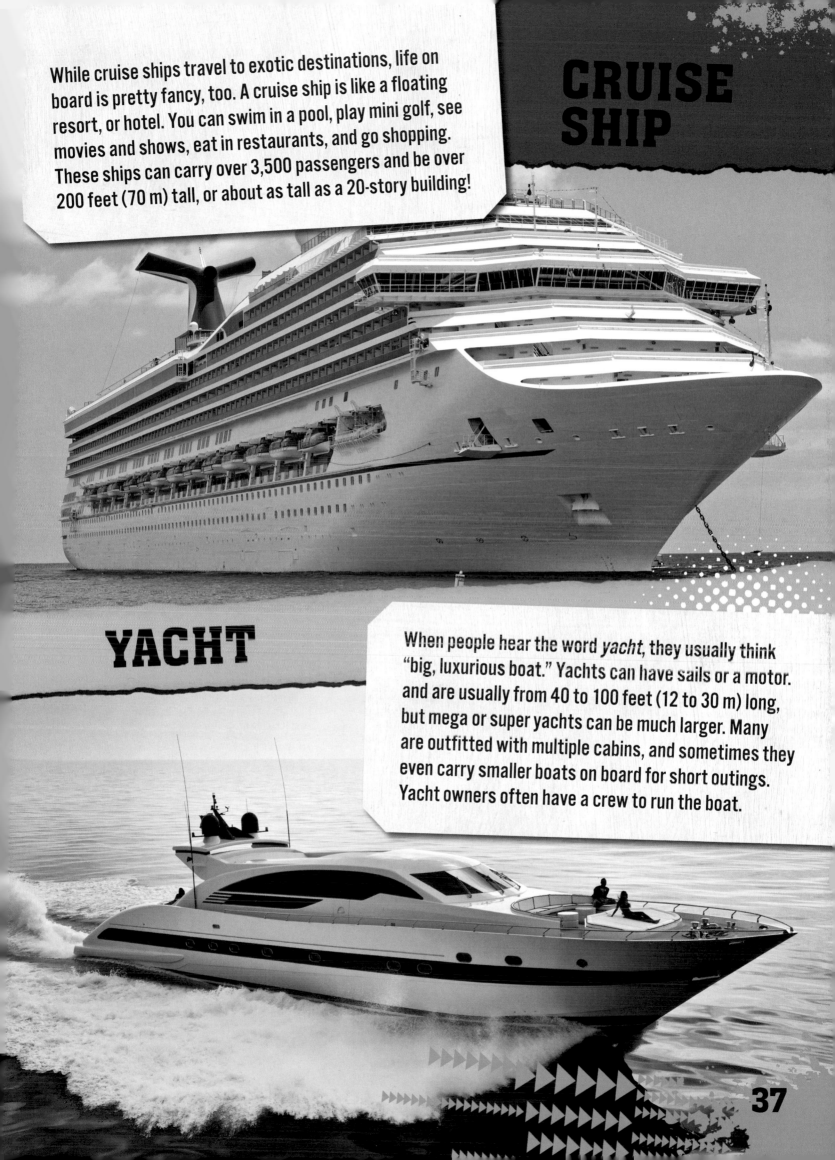

While cruise ships travel to exotic destinations, life on board is pretty fancy, too. A cruise ship is like a floating resort, or hotel. You can swim in a pool, play mini golf, see movies and shows, eat in restaurants, and go shopping. These ships can carry over 3,500 passengers and be over 200 feet (70 m) tall, or about as tall as a 20-story building!

CRUISE SHIP

YACHT

When people hear the word *yacht*, they usually think "big, luxurious boat." Yachts can have sails or a motor. and are usually from 40 to 100 feet (12 to 30 m) long, but mega or super yachts can be much larger. Many are outfitted with multiple cabins, and sometimes they even carry smaller boats on board for short outings. Yacht owners often have a crew to run the boat.

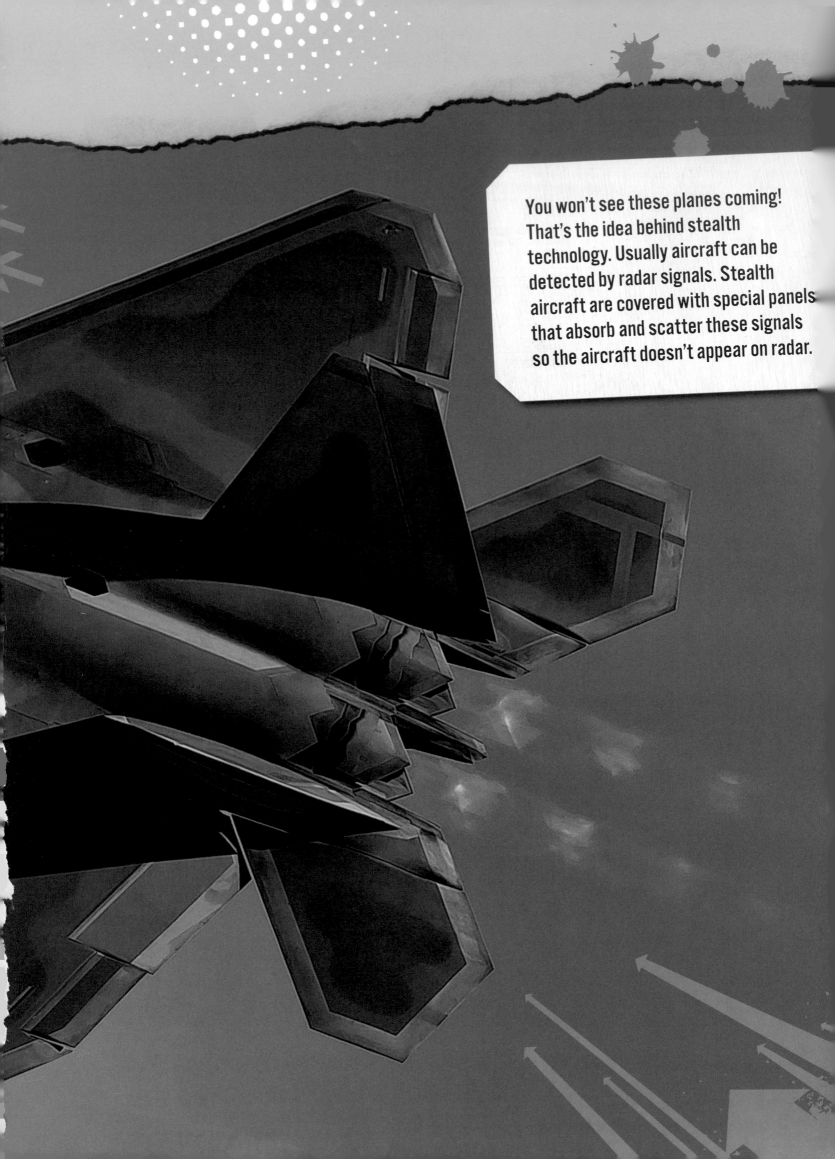

You won't see these planes coming! That's the idea behind stealth technology. Usually aircraft can be detected by radar signals. Stealth aircraft are covered with special panels that absorb and scatter these signals so the aircraft doesn't appear on radar.

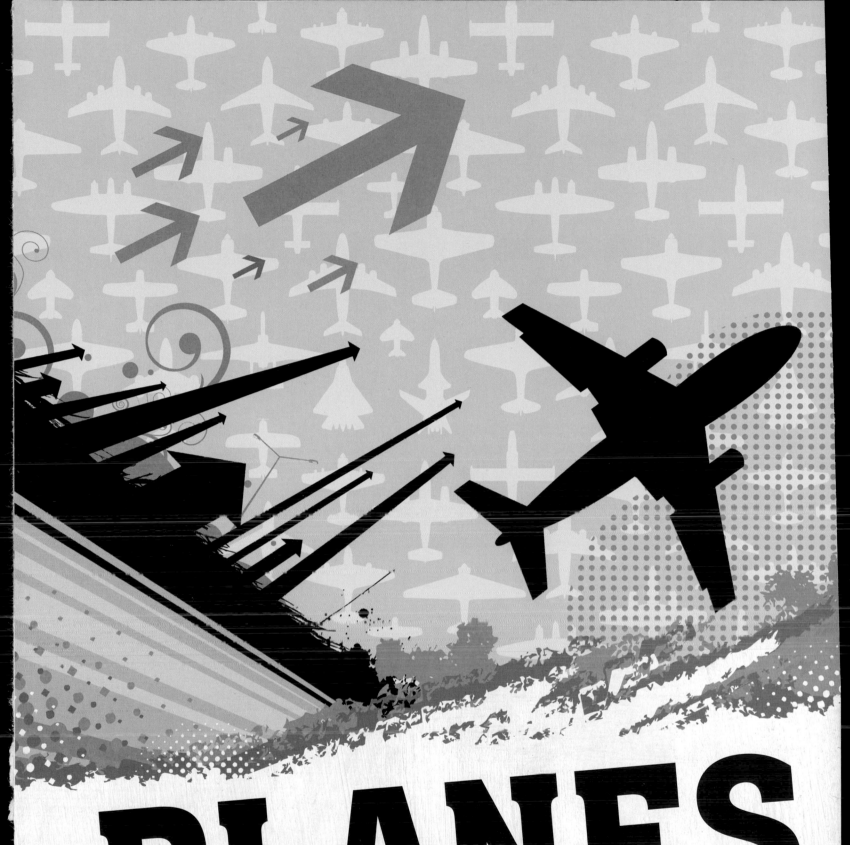

PLANES

Birds have always been our inspiration to fly. Inventors based their first glider designs on studies of birds. In 1903, Orville Wright became the first man to fly. It lasted 12 seconds! That's not much of a journey compared to today's planes, but engineers today still look to birds for design inspiration.

STEALTH AIRCRAFT

Their shape reduces noise and air turbulence, which also helps keep these aircraft from being detected as they approach.

CARGO PLANE

Cargo planes look so big and heavy, you might wonder how they fly. The body of the plane sits low to make it easy to load and unload cargo, or goods. Some cargo planes are big enough to carry another plane inside!

Cargo planes have huge doors on the side, in the back, or in the front nose (which flips up) to help load goods.

SOLAR-POWERED AIRCRAFT

Solar energy is power that comes from the light of the sun. Solar cells collect the sun's light and turn it into electricity. Solar-powered planes are coated with solar cells and are usually extremely lightweight. A solar-powered plane covered with 12,000 solar cells recently flew for over 24 hours, even through the dark of night.

Airplanes are able to fly because thrust—or the energy that moves a plane forward—helps the plane generate lift, or the force that moves a plane up into the air. This plane uses propellers to create thrust. Propeller, or prop, planes are quieter and use less fuel than jet-engine planes.

PROPELLER AIRPLANE

PRIVATE JET

Some private jets are equipped with features such as a den for watching television, a kitchen, and a bedroom.

Sometimes called business jets, or bizjets, these small jet planes carry fewer people than commercial jets.

COMMERCIAL JET

Today, some commercial jet planes can carry more than 500 passengers.

A jet plane, or jet, gets its name from the powerful jet engines that create the thrust to move the plane forward. Jets can fly at very high altitudes, about 33,000 to 49,000 feet (10,000 to 15,000 m). Commercial jets carry people and goods all over the world.

P-51 MUSTANG FIGHTER

During World War II, these sleek fighters escorted bombers deep into enemy territory. They are credited with shooting down 4,950 enemy aircraft. Today, you might see one of these speedy, agile planes at an air show.

SR-71 BLACKBIRD

Although this military jet isn't flown anymore, it still holds the record as the fastest air-breathing (a type of jet engine) manned aircraft. These awesome jets operated at very high altitudes—up to 80,000 feet (25,000 m)—and superfast speeds. The SR-71 Blackbird exceeded Mach 3, or three times the speed of sound. That's about 3,000 feet (914 m) per second!

MULTIROLE COMBAT AIRCRAFT

Some models, such as the F-35, even include stealth capabilities.

Different types of military planes are designed for different uses, or roles. Fighter planes are air-to-air combat specialists. Bomber planes target positions on the ground. Multirole combat aircraft do both.

F/A-18 HORNET

The letters F/A mean this is a fighter or attack jet. The Navy uses this jet as an escort fighter, so it flies alongside other planes to support them. But the F/A-18 is probably best known as the type of fighter used by the Blue Angels Flight Demonstration Squadron.

X-PLANES

Both the X-29, with its forward-swept wings, and the X-35 (inset), with its tailless design, were developed to test how plane structures affect maneuverability.

X-planes are as cool as they sound—X stands for "experimental." In 1946, NASA started building planes to test out new technologies. Some planes were top secret, but others are well known among plane enthusiasts. Why were X-planes so special? They were among the first to break the sound barrier and to fly at extremely high altitudes.

SUPERSONIC TRANSPORT

Traveling at Mach 2, or twice the speed of sound, these supersonic planes (called SST for short) were used as commercial planes that allowed passengers to fly long distances in half the time. They are no longer in use because they were very noisy, producing huge sonic booms in flight. However, researchers continue to work on new models that will overcome their drawbacks.

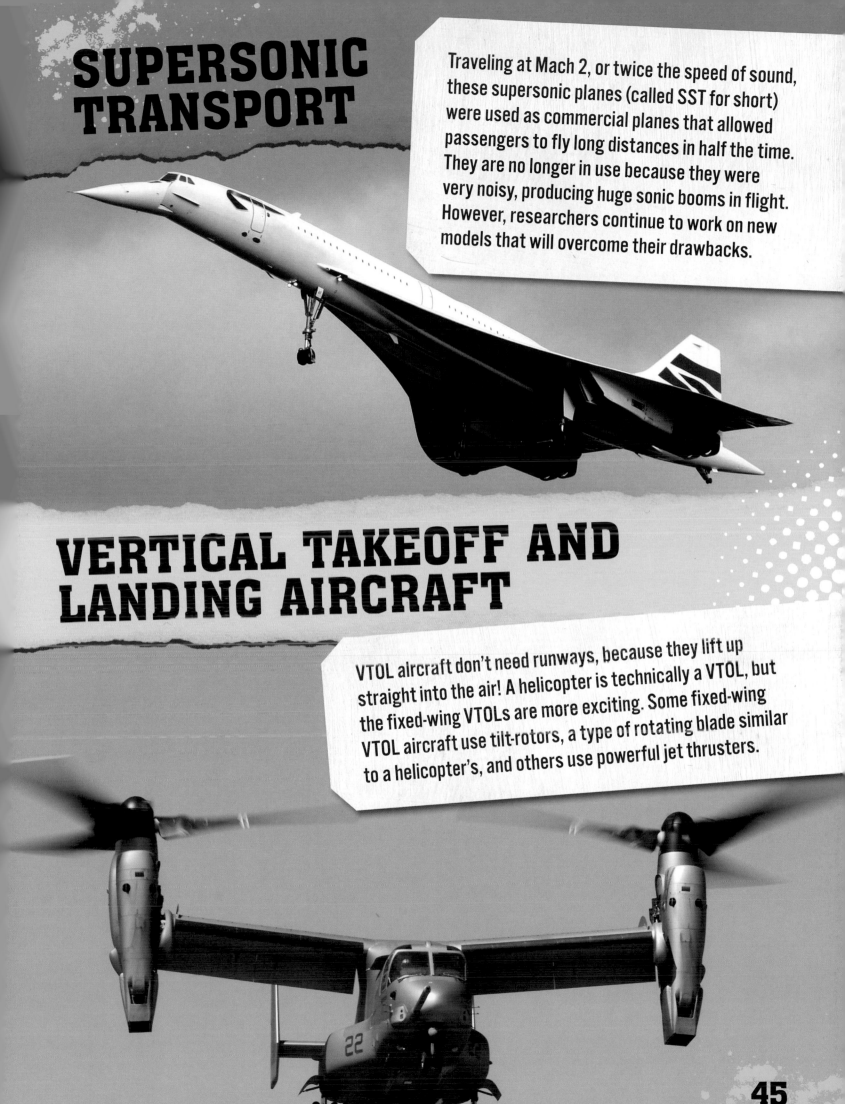

VERTICAL TAKEOFF AND LANDING AIRCRAFT

VTOL aircraft don't need runways, because they lift up straight into the air! A helicopter is technically a VTOL, but the fixed-wing VTOLs are more exciting. Some fixed-wing VTOL aircraft use tilt-rotors, a type of rotating blade similar to a helicopter's, and others use powerful jet thrusters.

FLOATPLANE

In place of wheels for landing, this plane has pontoons. Pontoons are floats that allow the plane to rest on the water. A floatplane takes off and lands on water.

CROP DUSTER

When farmers need to spread seeds, fertilizer, or pesticides over large areas, they call on crop dusters. Pilots fly these small, light planes low to the ground. Special equipment sprays the material on the fields as they fly over.

Air thermals are columns of warm, rising air. Birds such as hawks and eagles ride these air thermals—and so do gliders! These extremely lightweight planes have no engine. A tow plane pulls it up into the air. Then the sailplane unhooks from the tow plane and off it soars . . . just like a bird!

GLIDER (SAILPLANE)

BIPLANE

Biplanes are named for their two stacked wings. The double wings allow these planes to have smaller wingspans (the distance from wingtip to wingtip). A smaller wingspan lets a plane move around in tight spaces. Today, biplanes perform barrel rolls, dives, loops, and other crazy stunts at air shows.

HELICOPTER

Whump! Whump Whump! As the rotors, or blades, on the top of a helicopter whirl around and around, they lift the helicopter from the ground. Helicopters can take off and land going straight up or straight down. They can also fly backwards and sideways, and even hover in midair.

ZEPPELIN NT

It may look like an enormous, tube-shaped balloon, but a Zeppelin NT is actually an aircraft that is lighter than air! Its lightweight frame is wrapped in thick laminate and filled with nonflammable helium. So, in a way, it is like a balloon. Except that it's 246 feet (75 m) long, and has an engine and a driver!